Need to Know
Heroin

Sean Connolly

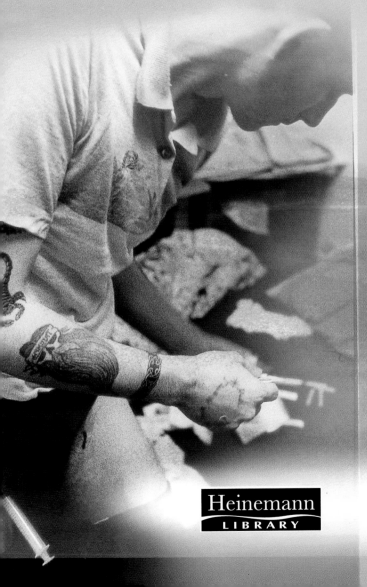

Heinemann
LIBRARY

www.heinemann.co.uk
visit our website to find out more information about **Heinemann Library** books.

To order:
☎ Phone 44 (0) 1865 888066
🖷 Send a fax to 44 (0) 1865 314091
💻 Visit the Heinemann Bookshop at www.heinemann.co.uk to browse our catalogue and order online.

First published in Great Britain by Heinemann Library, Halley Court, Jordan Hill, Oxford OX2 8EJ,
a division of Reed Educational and Professional Publishing Ltd.

Heinemann is a registered trademark of Reed Educational & Professional Publishing Limited.

Oxford Melbourne Auckland Johannesburg Blantyre Gaborone Ibadan Portsmouth NH (USA) Chicago

Designed by M2 Graphic Design
Printed in Hong Kong / China
Originated by Ambassador Litho Ltd.

04 03 02 01
10 9 8 7 6 5 4 3 2

ISBN 0431 097747

British Library Cataloguing in Publication Data
Sean Connolly
Heroin – (Need to know)
1. Heroin – Juvenile literature 2. Heroin habit – Juvenile literature
I. Title 362.2'93

Acknowledgements
The Publishers would like to thank the following for permission to reproduce photographs:
Camera Press: pg.24, pg.46; David Hoffman: pg.5, pg.11, pg.51; Frank Spooner: pg.28; Janine Wiedel:
pg.23; Magnum Photos: pg.29, pg.45, Wylie Donovan pg.9, Michael Nichols pg.34, pg.35, Griffiths pg.36,
Patrick King pg.37, Gilles Press pg.49; Mary Evans Picture Library: pg.18, pg.19; Network: Gideon Mendel
pg.17; Photofusion: Nicky Johnson pg.42; Redferns: William Gotlieb pg.22; Rex Features: pg.6, pg.7, pg.11,
pg.13, pg.15, pg.21, pg.25, pg.33, pg.40, pg.43, Jon Blum pg.31, Action Press pg.39; Science Photo
Library: pg.47; The Stock Market: pg.26, pg.27.

Every effort has been made to contact copyright holders of any material reproduced in this book.
Any omissions will be rectified in subsequent printings if notice is given to the publisher.

Any words appearing in the text in bold, **like this**, are explained in the Glossary.

Contents

Introduction

Heroin is a drug of extremes. For many people it is the most feared drug, while for others its powerful 'high' offers the most dramatic way of escaping the cares and boredom of everyday life. It is the drug that immediately springs to mind when people talk about **dependence** and drug-related crime, and it forms the backbone of drug-treatment programmes in Britain and many other countries.

A tempting offer

Just why do people take a drug like heroin, if it has so many associations with illness and death? Although the answer seems complex, it can be reduced to one word – escape. Heroin does not promise to lift the spirits or to find new ways of looking at life. Instead it offers a chance to retreat from life, wrapped in a cocoon of artificial comfort while the drug takes effect. Gradually, as people become used to the drug, this sense of comfort fades and is replaced by a feeling of relief that they have found another dose – and it becomes harder still to return to the life that was so boring and difficult in the first place.

This sounds depressing – and it is. Very few people who are deeply involved with heroin find any pleasure in the drug – they are driven by the urge to have more of it simply to feel 'normal'.

A familiar story

Heroin abuse is a serious modern problem, although humans have been sampling the effects of its raw ingredient – the opium poppy – for more than 4000 years. The urge to escape reality obviously has deep roots, and has been recorded by writers throughout history. This means of escape was as familiar to the characters in Homer's *Odyssey* as it was in Irvine Welsh's account of modern Edinburgh, *Trainspotting*, 2700 years later. The core drug is pretty much the same but the means of taking it – and the dangers involved – have become more varied.

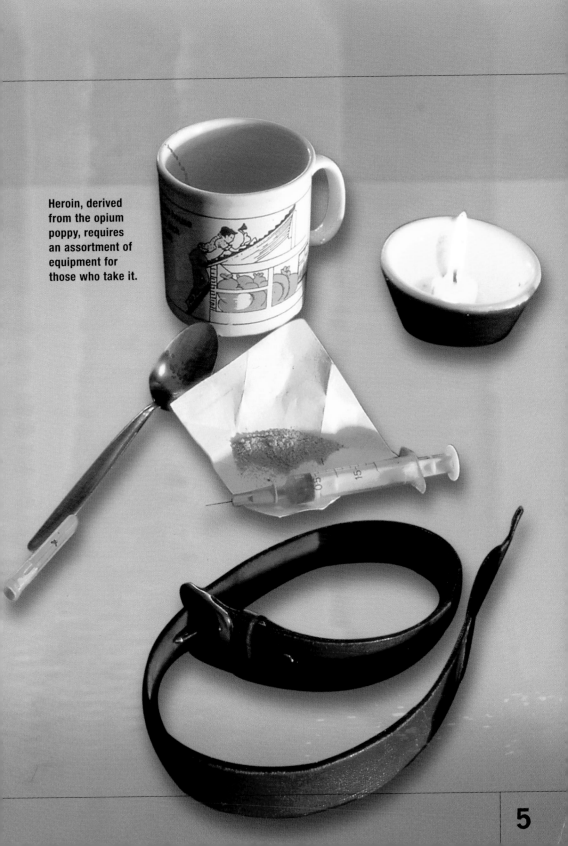

Heroin, derived from the opium poppy, requires an assortment of equipment for those who take it.

What is heroin?

Heroin is one of a group of drugs known as **opiates**, which means that they are derived from the opium poppy. Opium is the dried 'milk' of this poppy and it contains two very effective painkillers – codeine and morphine. Heroin is simply morphine that has had an extra chemical group added to it, in order to make it more **soluble** in fat. This addition enables heroin to enter the brain faster. Interestingly, once heroin enters the brain it is converted back into morphine.

Pure heroin is a white powder – its street nickname is 'white lady' – but by the time people buy it on the street it is light brown, leading to another of its nicknames – 'brown'. Between production and eventual purchase the **purity** decreases from 100 per cent to somewhere between 20 and 60 per cent. It is often mixed or 'cut' with paracetemol, sugar or other **tranquillizers**, so that the dealer can make the original supply of heroin go further – and get more money in the process. Use of heroin can lead to real trouble on many different fronts. It is possible to die of a heroin **overdose**, particularly if the drug is very pure.

Mixing heroin with other drugs, including alcohol, can lead to dangerous medical side-effects. **Injecting** heroin also runs the risk of **HIV** infection or **hepatitis** because heroin users often share needles and thus pass on infection. Heroin is also powerfully **addictive**, both physically and mentally, and it can be extremely hard to break the cycle of **dependence**. The cost of getting supplies of heroin can cause serious money problems, and many users turn to crime to get money for the drug.

"Smack by name, then it literally smacks you in the face."

(Heroin user at HM Prison Wealstun)

A heroin user opens a paper 'wrap' containing a single dose of the drug.

What is heroin?

Into the cocoon

Once it has been taken heroin is quickly absorbed into the bloodstream and soon reaches the brain. First-time users report different effects from the drug. Some people feel little or no effect from their first 'hit' of heroin. Others find the experience immediately unpleasant and feel nauseous. Most people, though, get a warm feeling which starts in the belly and then spreads across all of the body, seeming to wrap them in a glow of well being. This warm, dreamy feeling is very comforting – responsibilities seem to drift away as the user 'returns to the womb'. Other users describe it as being wrapped in a cocoon.

Many of the nicknames for heroin are accurate indicators of the drug's appearance or its effects. Apart from visually descriptive terms such as 'white lady' and 'brown', heroin is also known as 'smack'. The term is appropriate, because when heroin is smoked or **injected** the effects hit hard and suddenly.

How people take heroin

Heroin, like most **opiates**, is easily absorbed into the body through many different routes, largely because it dissolves in fatty substances and can cross into the body's cells. One route that is not very effective is through the stomach, so very few people swallow heroin. However, it can be sniffed (or 'snorted'), smoked or injected. When sniffed, heroin is absorbed into the bloodstream through the nose. If it is smoked, heroin enters the bloodstream very quickly through the lining of the lungs. One method of smoking heroin is called 'chasing the dragon'. This process involves heating the heroin powder and inhaling the fumes through a small tube. This is the method that introduces many users to regular use of the drug.

Regular users often inject heroin directly into the bloodstream through a vein. As with smoking heroin, the effects are almost immediate except that they are stronger since none of the drug is 'lost' before entering the bloodstream. Before injecting it, a heroin user must dissolve the drug in a liquid.

Is heroin addictive?

Even people who are, in general, unfamiliar with drugs know that heroin is **addictive**. But just what does this mean? And what about the stories that people can get 'hooked' on the drug after just one session?

Defining the problem

Several medical texts define **addiction** as 'the repetitive, compulsive use of a substance that occurs despite negative consequences to the user'. Drug workers prefer to use the word **dependence** rather than addiction. There are two types of dependence – psychological and physical. Certain chemicals in the brain, which are nicknamed the 'pleasure circuits', are activated by drugs that produce psychological dependency. Heroin is one of those drugs.

Tracing the 'pleasure circuit'

Heroin produces psychological dependence because the brain feels enjoyment during the **rush** of a heroin high, and the 'pleasure circuits' associate this enjoyment with the heroin. This process works in other, non drug-related ways as well.

For example, someone might enjoy the taste of a freshly-baked cake so much that the smell of another cake prepares the brain to re-create the experience. Scientists are only now beginning to understand what happens chemically in this process: heroin and certain other drugs (including alcohol) release a 'messenger' called **dopamine** which rushes the pleasure message through this part of the brain. In experiments conducted with rats, the test animals performed tasks in order to receive drugs that had triggered dopamine; when the dopamine circuits were destroyed the rats would not perform tasks to receive the same drugs.

Reinforcing this psychological dependence is the fact that a regular heroin user will almost always be associated with others who are dependent on the drug. It is hard to break out of a social pattern that sees the same faces taking the same drug, day in and day out.

A heroin injector mixes the drugs with water in a teaspoon, heats it until it dissolves, and then draws it into the **syringe.**

Is heroin addictive?

The physical side

Tied in with physical **dependence** is the idea of **tolerance**, or the way that the body becomes accustomed to a drug and begins to need more of it to produce the original effect. Heroin takes this process a step further. After several weeks of regular use, which usually means increasing amounts, the pleasure of the first heroin highs is replaced by relief at getting hold of the drug.

By this stage, the heroin user is truly hooked and there is little or no pleasure in taking the drug – only the blocking out of pain that develops when the body begins crying out for another dose. With tolerance and the need for increased amounts of heroin, the user tends to progress through different methods of taking the drug. Snorting or smoking heroin, which provides a high for someone new to the drug, is less effective at getting heroin into the bloodstream than **injecting**, so the dependent user usually moves on to needles and **syringes**.

Other side-effects

Regular use of heroin introduces a range of other health side-effects. Strictly speaking these are not the result of dependence, but a dependent user will normally have most of these symptoms. The greatest risk is contracting **hepatitis** or **HIV**. Both of these conditions are passed on in the exchange of bodily fluids and there is a serious risk of contracting them if people injecting heroin share needles or syringes.

The heroin 'lifestyle' leaves little room for eating and sleeping properly, so users are often run down and open to other infections. Heroin also acts on the digestive system, leading to constipation and some stomach ailments. It also affects the **respiratory** system, leaving users prone to pneumonia and bronchitis.

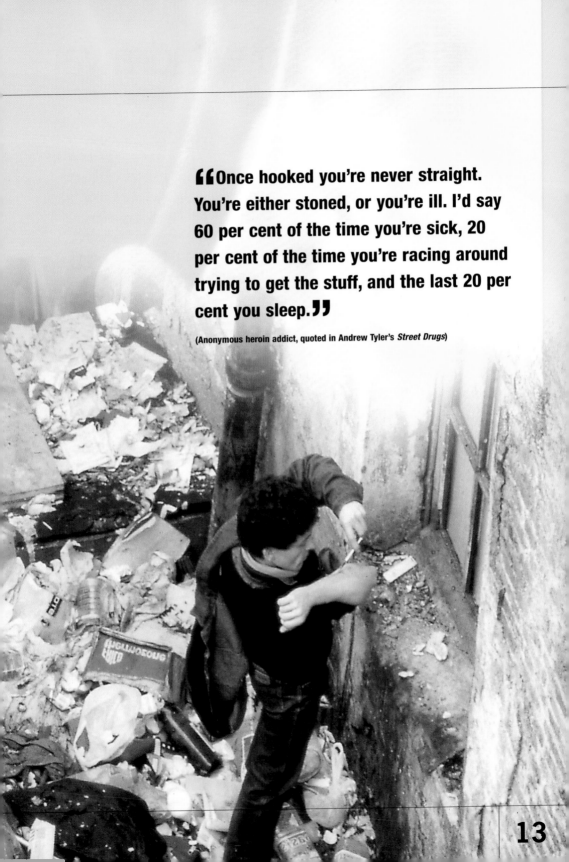

❝Once hooked you're never straight. You're either stoned, or you're ill. I'd say 60 per cent of the time you're sick, 20 per cent of the time you're racing around trying to get the stuff, and the last 20 per cent you sleep.❞

(Anonymous heroin addict, quoted in Andrew Tyler's *Street Drugs*)

Overdose and withdrawal

To **overdose** means to take more of a drug (such as heroin) than the body is **tolerant** to. In the case of heroin, this unexpectedly large amount can be taken if a new supply of the drug has a greater **purity** than the user's normal supply has. The overdose can happen within minutes but more commonly takes from one to twelve hours. Breathing becomes slow and irregular and the skin turns blue as the blood pressure drops, then the user falls into a **coma**. Death, if it occurs from an overdose, is the result of **respiratory** failure or complications with the heart. A person need not be **dependent** on heroin to overdose – it is the unexpectedly large dose that does the damage.

Cold turkey

The other main aspect of heroin dependence is well known – **withdrawal**, also known as 'cold turkey'. If someone stops taking heroin after prolonged regular use they feel dramatically ill. This reaches a peak about three days after the last heroin was taken. Symptoms are similar to those of a particularly bad case of flu – fever, aching limbs, sweating, restlessness, cramps and **insomnia**. The skin becomes terribly itchy and develops bumps resembling goose bumps (hence the term 'cold turkey'). In addition, the user feels anxious and isolated and often has unsettling waking dreams.

The symptoms recede after about a week or ten days but the feeling of weakness and loss of well being can last for several months. By finally 'riding it out' through these last stages of withdrawal the user overcomes most of the effects of physical dependence. However, many users return to the drug even after going through the experience. Therefore, scientists now believe that the psychological dependence is a more powerful factor in keeping heroin users hooked on the drug.

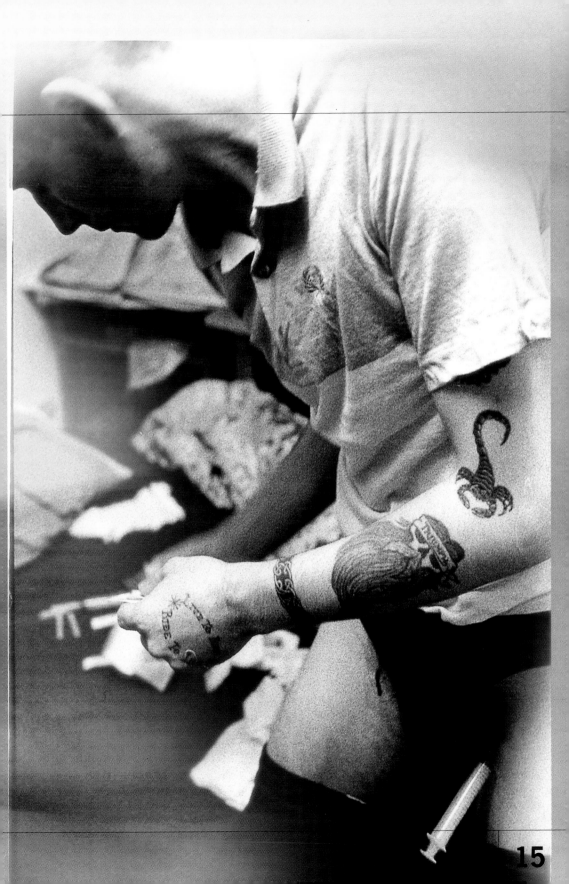

A widespread problem

Heroin abuse is a growing problem, and the 1990s saw one of the biggest increases in its use. Some statistics indicate the scale of the increase. In 1991 there were 4883 heroin **addicts** reported to the UK Home Office. The 1994 figure was more than twice that number – 10,067. Unofficial 'word of mouth' estimates by drug workers confirmed this overall rise in the use of heroin in that short period, and suggest that it has continued since then.

Increased supplies

A pair of alarming statistics provide one – of many – reasons for this rise in the use of heroin. In 1991 British police and customs officials seized 490 kilograms of heroin. The amount seized had risen to 1390 kilograms by 1995, almost trebling in four years. Heroin seizures are rising sharply with 1997 seeing nearly double the previous numbers of seizures at 12,474 (weighing 2235 kilograms). Britain is not alone – the United States and Australia have also seen a rise in the amount of heroin being smuggled in across the borders.

These increased amounts of heroin were almost certainly linked to the rise in the number of addicts. Quite simply, having more heroin in the country meant that the drug spread further afield, but also that the price went down. The **influx** of the drug has had other effects as well, which made the heroin problem more difficult to deal with. Hitherto seen as primarily a drug of the inner city – where unemployment and poor social facilities drive some people to use the drug – heroin use has now been cropping up all over Britain. Rural areas have reported a sharp increase in heroin use throughout the 1990s. At the same time, a greater number of young people have become exposed to the drug.

Similar trends have been reported in the United States, Canada, Australia and many other countries, where the increase in supply – coupled with greater **purity** and lower prices – have sparked an increase in heroin use. The drug is no longer confined to the more rundown districts of New York, Toronto or Sydney, which means that the problem of heroin use can no longer be 'pigeon-holed'.

“We’ve got something serious on our hands and we need to do something about it now. If we don’t, it will become an epidemic.”

(The West Yorkshire drug agency Unit 51, reporting in 1995)

A lengthy history

Although heroin itself is a comparatively recent development – being about 125 years old – **opiates** have played a part in human history for thousands of years. The opium poppy grows across central Asia, and there are records of the Assyrian and Babylonian civilizations using opium about 4000 years ago. The ancient Greeks and Romans also prized opium for its power to relax and calm people. The Greek goddess Demeter, for example, used opium to soothe her sorrows. Morpheus, the Greek god of dreams (who also lends his name to the drug morphine), was often depicted with a handful of opium poppies.

The ancient Greeks linked their god of dreams, Morpheus (below), with opium poppies. Opium use became more widespread in the nineteenth century, when users would smoke it in secret dens (right).

Arab traders introduced opiates to China between AD600 and AD900. It was in China that the **recreational** use of opiates grew over the following centuries. Similarly, Europeans began to use opiates, both for medicinal purposes and for pleasure, in the Middle Ages. A new wave of opium arrived in Britain in the 1500s. Mixed with alcohol and spices, the drug became known as 'laudanum', which is a Latin word meaning 'worthy of praise'.

A trading see-saw

By the mid-nineteenth century laudanum (in Europe) and opium itself (in Asia, especially China) were increasingly common. Many English writers, including Thomas de Quincey, Samuel Taylor Coleridge, Charles Dickens and Elizabeth Barrett Browning, claimed that the drug inspired them. Working people also used opium at this time in England, adding it to a pint of beer and even giving it to children to help them sleep.

By the end of that century the British government began to worry about increased use of opium. From 1868 opiates could only be bought from pharmacies, although a **black market** trade meant users could still get supplies. Part of the problem arose due to the government's own trading plans, involving shipping opium to China. Chinese sailors arrived in London's docklands, and established 'opium dens' where people could smoke the drug in secrecy. At about the same time many Chinese immigrants to the United States brought their drug habits with them, causing alarm.

Modern refinements

The nineteenth century also saw the changes that would lead to the modern drug of heroin. In 1805 morphine, the major active ingredient in heroin, was first purified. Then, in 1853, the hypodermic **syringe** was invented, making it possible to **inject** a liquid form of the drug. This was developed as a medical tool, so that the drug could be given more easily by doctors and nurses. In 1874 German scientists modified the drug morphine to make it even stronger. This new form of morphine was called *heroisch*, meaning 'powerful' in German. *Heroisch* was not the same as what we now call heroin; the final advance came in 1898. Scientists working for the Swiss chemical company Bayer added an extra chemical group to morphine to make it more **soluble** in fat, so that it would enter the brain faster. This finally produced heroin.

Dealing with trouble

Heroin was hailed as a remarkable painkiller as soon as it was invented. It was supplied to hospitals and medical surgeries.

A form of heroin known as diamorphine is still given to thousands of cancer patients each year, as well as to women during childbirth. However, since it was first developed the extra power of heroin has also attracted non-medical users.

In the early part of the twentieth century more and more people began taking heroin, and many became **addicted** to it. The controls on the trade in **opiates** were strengthened in the 1920s. Heroin was made illegal for non-medical uses, both in the United States and in the UK. Britain, however, did not ban the drug altogether. The government set up a system whereby **addicts** could have controlled amounts of heroin **prescribed** by a doctor.

Classical past

The great poet of ancient Greece, Homer, wrote his epic poem *The Odyssey* in about 700BC. In it he referred to a mysterious drug nepenthes, which 'lulled all pain and gave forgetfulness of grief. No one that swallowed this dissolved in wine could shed a single tear that day, even for the death of his mother or father.' There is some debate about exactly what nepenthes was, but the effects described are almost identical to those of opium, which was well known in Greece at that time.

Despite international attempts to curb the heroin trade, the opium poppy harvest remains a major money earner in many parts of the world.

The modern era

With its use banned – or virtually
banned – in most countries, heroin
became an **underground** drug from
the 1920s onwards. **Addicts** and
casual users got their drugs through
illegal sources. Secret laboratories
produced heroin, and a complex
network of **drug traffickers** kept most
countries supplied with the drug.

The new wave

By now heroin was seen as a
dangerous drug. The public had
become aware of the risk of
dependence and **overdose**. The
1960s, however, saw an increase in
drug use generally. Many people who
had tried 'softer' drugs such as
cannabis were curious about heroin.
If some of the 'scare stories' about
cannabis were wrong, as they came
to believe, then perhaps the even
scarier stories about heroin were
also exaggerations. Many people
who tried heroin at that time
either found that they didn't like
it, or simply turned away after
trying it once or twice. Others,
however, got sucked into a
pattern of dependence and
self-perpetuating **addiction**.

The jazz saxophone player
Charlie Parker (below) was one
of many musicians whose lives
were damaged by heroin use. The
same problem arose among US
soldiers during the Vietnam war
a decade later.

These addicts, plus many who had a longer heroin history, found new ways of ensuring a supply.

Some of the heroin reaching British streets in the 1960s had been obtained through the official 'system', which allowed heroin to be **prescribed** by a doctor if a user could not face life without the drug. Some users managed to get hold of surplus supplies of the drug and sold it to other users.

In 1968 the UK government tightened controls on the drug so that only a few specialist doctors could prescribe heroin.

Refuge for the poor

Today's pattern of heroin use dates back to the early 1970s. Like nowadays, users were a mixture of the curious and the dependent. Since then the largest group – and one that is still growing – has been people from **disadvantaged** backgrounds. There were many economic upheavals in the 1970s, which left large portions of the population without work and without much hope of ever finding a job. For such people, heroin has become a way of coping with a life that is boring and holds no promise of fun or excitement.

Who takes heroin?

Like other **derivatives** of opium, heroin's strength is its ability to make pain seem unimportant. At the same time it produces a powerful sense of well being. In this respect it differs from **stimulants** such as amphetamines and cocaine, which 'lift' users and encourage them to be more active or talkative. Also, compared to **hallucinogenic** drugs such as LSD, it does not send the user through a kaleidoscope of intense sensations and emotions. Many heroin users describe the effects of the drug as being 'wrapped in cotton wool'.

A dead end?

The numbing effects of heroin are hardly what thrill-seekers are looking for. Instead, the people who are often drawn to heroin are those whose lives seem intolerable – the long-term unemployed, the poor and other **disadvantaged** people. For them it offers a break from reality, a time when time itself doesn't matter.

The use of heroin is seen as a problem in its own right – with its risks of **overdose**, poisoning and **HIV** – but it is also a reflection of a wider social problem. Although high-profile heroin users such as Kurt Cobain or Keith Richards grab some headlines, the greater number of heroin users are young and jobless. People in the most rundown inner-city districts are the ones who will be tempted to drift into heroin use.

Mixed signals

The use of heroin among the young has become a serious problem in Britain and the United States. Most surveys suggest an alarming and depressing increase in the numbers of young heroin users. Added to this, people are beginning to take the drug at a much earlier age than even ten years ago.

Part of the problem lies in the image of heroin use. The film *Trainspotting*, based on Irvine Welsh's hard-hitting novel about heroin users in Scotland, opened in 1996. Although it pulled no punches about the negative side of the heroin scene, the film succeeded almost too well in showing the attractive side of its characters.

The central character, Renton, was played by Ewan McGregor, who was no one's idea of a haggard **junkie**. The film was extremely popular around the world, prompting many fashion and style magazines to talk about 'heroin chic'. Almost overnight, heroin **addiction** took on a high profile. Painfully thin models, working for leading fashion designers, posed in what looked like wrecked back streets. Heroin, once seen solely as a 'loser's drug', suddenly had glamour.

A heroin user shows little interest in the outside world, retreating instead into a numbing cocoon.

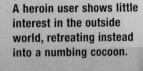

Who takes heroin?

A day in the life of a heroin user

While some people take heroin occasionally and manage to cope with life, the picture is very different for those who are **dependent** on the drug. For them, heroin becomes their life. The constant need to keep supplied creates a distinct 'sameness' to their existence.

From the moment a heroin-dependent person wakes up, finding the next **fix** becomes their main concern. This means getting hold of money, so the user often turns to petty crime such as burglary or shoplifting. Then he goes looking for a dealer, usually one who has had supplies in the past. There is little life outside of this cycle of seeking and finding the fix. Sadly, many of the other people he meets during the day – including the dealer – are in the same position.

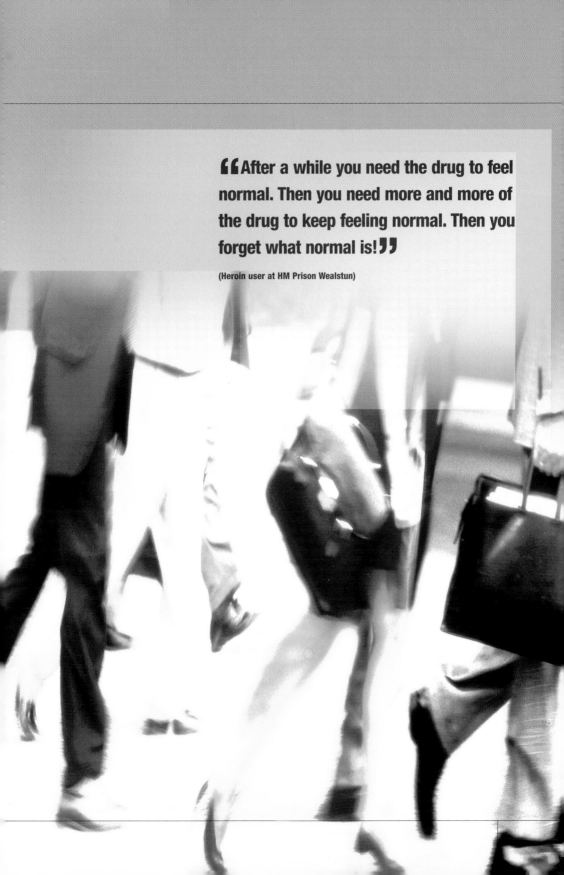

"After a while you need the drug to feel normal. Then you need more and more of the drug to keep feeling normal. Then you forget what normal is!"

(Heroin user at HM Prison Wealstun)

Getting hold of heroin

Lou Reed's 1960s group, the Velvet Underground, recorded a powerful song called 'Waiting for the Man'. The man referred to in the title was a heroin dealer, and the song conjured up images of a heroin-**dependent** user's bleak life, constantly looking for the next **fix**. Nineteenth-century writers such as the poets Coleridge and Baudelaire saw **opiates** as a spur to creativity. Lou Reed's song, like the work of the novelist William Burroughs (author of the novel *Junkie*), captures the modern view of heroin – a depressing companion which drains the mind of any thoughts except where the next fix will come from.

A car radio seems like easy pickings for a heroin user desperate to get money for his next fix.

Black economy

With heroin illegal except in the most exceptional circumstances, users must get supplies through the **black market**. The illegal trade in heroin is worth billions, but most of that money goes to the large-scale importers of the drug. At street level, the position is usually different. A supplier, or 'dealer', will profit from the sale of heroin, but very often the profit simply goes to feed the dealer's own heroin habit.

Heavily dependent users rarely have ready cash of their own. The problem is finding regular amounts to pay for each fix.

It is at this stage that heroin becomes closely linked to rising crime levels, as users often break into houses or cars and sometimes even rob shops.

Police can usually recognize the evidence of a drug-related robbery. A 'professional thief' usually has targets in mind before the robbery, and therefore leaves very few traces behind. In a drug-related robbery, however, property is usually ransacked as the drug user searches desperately for something that might be worth money if resold.

Firing blanks

For some people who have become dependent on heroin, the very act of **injecting** offers some form of comfort – even without heroin. A person with such a fixation will often fill a **syringe** with warm water and inject it into a vein. The injection, of course, has no real effect, but it reminds the user of the comfort that a heroin injection would supply.

Wider effects

Heroin affects more than just the single person who uses it regularly. The circumstances leading to heavy use can be varied, as can the responses from other family members, but the core problem is the same. A young person has had their field of vision narrowed so much by a drug that they cannot function without it.

Anger and confusion

It is quite common for the children of heroin-**dependent** parents to become dependent on the drug themselves. This is particularly true in areas worst hit by unemployment or poverty. The same lack of prospects that turned the parents to heroin are still there, twenty or thirty years later. Life becomes a depressing spiral in these circumstances, with no one able to see the problem with any sense of **perspective**.

It is a different problem for families with no history of heroin involvement. Parents often deal with the problem by avoiding it – simply because it seems too hard to believe. They need advice, but they might be too ashamed to approach counsellors or drug clinics. This lack of action – which amounts to ignoring the problem – also leads to a painful spiral. The only chance of a positive outcome arises when they, or friends of the user, face up to the problem. Ultimately, however, it is the user who must be prepared to join in any solution.

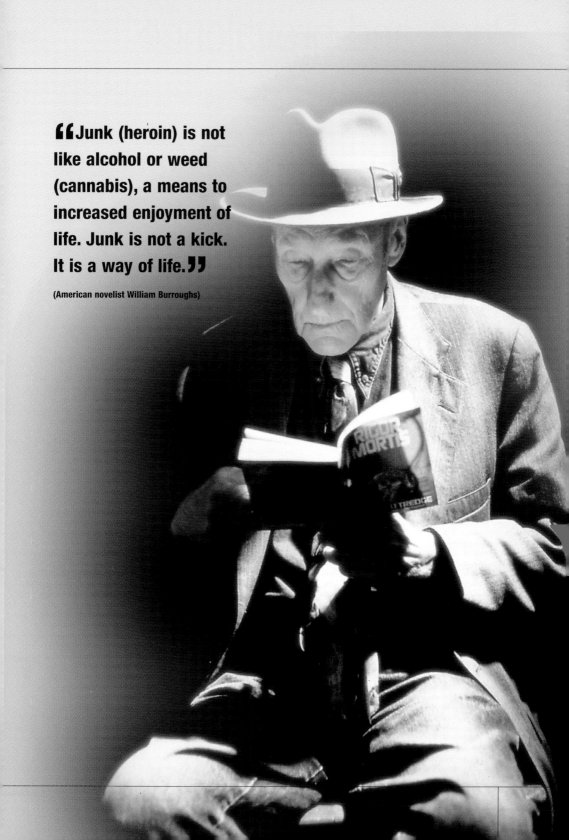

❝Junk (heroin) is not like alcohol or weed (cannabis), a means to increased enjoyment of life. Junk is not a kick. It is a way of life.❞

(American novelist William Burroughs)

Price and prevalence

One of the basic rules of economics is called the Law of Supply and Demand. Put simply, it means that the price of something rises or falls as a result of changes in either the amount of it available (the supply) or the amount people want to buy it (the demand). If supply increases faster than demand, then prices fall. If demand outpaces supply, then the prices go up.

Heroin is a good example of this law at work. The demand for the drug is rising, but the supply is rising much faster. As a result, many countries are facing a dangerous problem of heroin abuse, coupled with a falling price – which in turn makes it easier for new users to afford the drug. There are many reasons for the increase in heroin supplies. One of them is simply that recent years have seen good harvests of opium poppies in central and eastern Asia, the traditional suppliers of heroin. In addition, political events have played a part (see page 36), leading to a greater illegal trade in the drug.

The heroin that actually reaches the street now is much purer than it was even ten years ago, so that current users face an extra risk of **overdose** because their bodies are not expecting such a concentrated 'hit'.

Street prices

As a result of the extra supply, the price that heroin users pay for the drug has come down in real terms. The drug is usually sold in small packets of paper called 'wraps', which contain a specific weight of heroin – usually fractions of a gram. A wrap might contain 50 milligrams of heroin, about enough for one 'hit' for a new user, or perhaps 100 milligrams. The actual price works out at anywhere between £20 and £80 for a gram, depending on the location.

The heroin industry

NO DEALING !

NO HOLDING DRUGS
NO USING DRUGS

NO ALCOHOL
NO PETS

ANY OF THESE
CAN CLOSE THE CLINIC

We Love You

The heroin trade represents a huge worldwide industry, and in some respects it resembles other **commodities** such as coffee and cocoa in the way it reaches markets thousands of miles from its original source. Like coffee, the raw ingredient of heroin is grown and harvested. Then it is **processed**. The first stage of processing – for both coffee and heroin – is to dry the crop. For coffee, the process continues through a roasting stage and then either grinding or further processing for instant coffee. The process for heroin is similar, with an additional chemical stage at the end of the line. Morphine is extracted from the dried sap from the seed pods of opium poppies. It is this morphine – a powerful **opiate** in itself – that is the last stage before heroin is produced. Chemicals are added to the morphine to make it more **soluble** in fats, and the result is heroin.

Medical uses

It must be remembered that heroin was developed as a tool for medicine, not as a **recreational** drug. Doctors and **pharmaceutical** scientists in the late nineteenth century had been searching for an effective painkiller for people who had undergone major surgery or had painful illnesses such as cancer. The development of heroin in 1898 was hailed as a breakthrough in the medical world.

Heroin still occupies a place in medical science, in the role for which it was developed. In addition to the small amounts that doctors can **prescribe** to **dependent** heroin users in Britain under what is known as the 'system' (see pages 22–3), the drug is used in a variety of medical settings. It provides effective pain relief for sufferers from **terminal** cancer and other conditions that lead to prolonged, uninterrupted pain. A close relative of heroin, called diamorphine, is given to mothers during childbirth – again to relieve pain. These medical uses are all strictly controlled, to prevent the spread of heroin on to the **black market**.

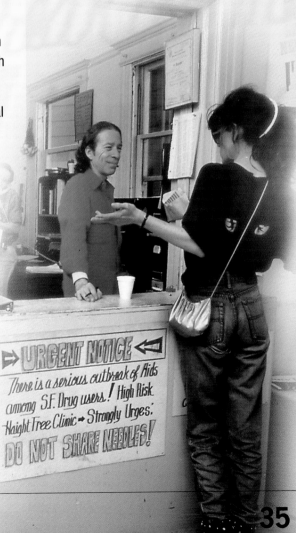

A San Francisco drug clinic warns of the dangers linked to injecting heroin and other drugs.

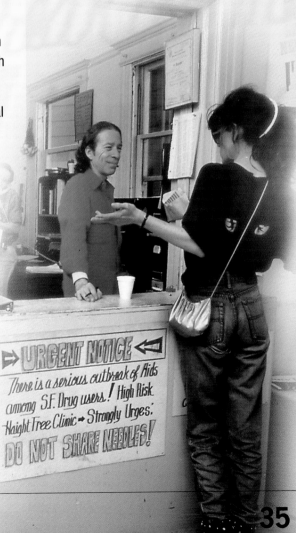

➡ URGENT NOTICE ⬅
There is a serious outbreak of Aids among S.F. Drug users ! High Risk Haight Tree Clinic ➡ Strongly Urges:
DO NOT SHARE NEEDLES!

The illegal trade

It is illegal to trade in opium or in any of its byproducts, which include heroin. However, the demand for heroin is so great that this illegal trade produces huge profits for those who are willing to risk getting caught. The heroin that reaches the streets of London or New York probably originated in a poppy field in Asia. Along the way, each link of the trading chain adds to the price. The last link, the dealers, make some profit but often only enough to feed their own heroin habit.

The 'other' heroin habit

One of the biggest problems in dealing with the heroin trade is that growing opium poppies helps poor Asian farmers earn money. Getting them to stop and to turn to other crops is difficult, for several reasons. The governments in many of the countries where the poppies are grown are weak. They could not contain the protests that would arise if farmers were forced away from poppy **cultivation**.

Substitute crops, grown instead of opium poppies, do not earn nearly as much money for these farmers.

Moreover, the regions where poppies are grown are usually remote and difficult to monitor. In these regions, opium poppy cultivation is part of the culture – indirectly, it forms a 'heroin habit' of its own.

The illegal trade in heroin begins in small villages in Southeast Asia, where many villages rely on income from supplying the drug.

Tackling the traffickers

Sensing that it is very difficult to prevent people from actually growing opium poppies – the raw material for heroin – governments around the world have turned their attention to dealing with **drug trafficking**. It is during the middle stage of the heroin trade, when it is **processed** and sent to different countries, that most of the illegal profits have been made.

In 1988 several countries signed the United Nations Convention against Illegal Traffic in Narcotic Drugs and **Psychotropic** Substances. This Convention set out guidelines for dealing with **money laundering**, the complicated method of turning drugs profits into legal money.

International agreements such as the UN Convention described above also confront the issue of controlling the chemicals that are used in processing opium and other plant-based substances into hard drugs such as heroin and cocaine.

The illegal trade

Economic threat

The whole issue of **drug trafficking** – in which heroin plays a large role – has had a huge effect on Europe in particular. Asia remains the source of most heroin but it is through Europe that the drug is distributed. The most recent rise in use of heroin and the corresponding drop in price took place in the early 1990s. This was a period of European upheaval anyway, for two main reasons.

The first was the collapse of the **communist** system in the former Soviet Union and other Eastern European countries. This change led to political instability across much of the region. Many people in the southern parts of the former Soviet Union turned to opium production as a source of income. Others, both in the former Soviet Union and in war-torn Yugoslavia, found that they could trade heroin for guns in areas where violence had taken hold.

The second reason had to do with the relaxation in 1992 of European **frontier** restrictions. This move was intended to enable the European Community to grow stronger. Unfortunately, the freer movement of people and goods through Europe also allowed drug smugglers an easier time in getting heroin from one country to another.

In the United States, the trade in heroin and other hard drugs is largely controlled by organized crime. These criminals are sophisticated in the way that they import the drugs as well as the way that they hide their profits through **money laundering**.

Spanish customs police arrest a suspected drug trafficker in the port of Cadiz. Large amounts of heroin can be smuggled into countries on high-speed boats, usually operating under the cover of darkness.

Legal matters

In Britain heroin and other **opiates** are controlled under the Misuse of Drugs Act 1971. It is illegal to possess or supply them to other people without a prescription. It is also illegal to produce, import or export these drugs, or to allow premises to be used for their production or supply. Similar laws exist in the United States, where the Drug Enforcement Agency (a federal agency) lists heroin among the most serious drugs of abuse in Schedule 1 of its drugs classification.

Possessing, using, making or selling heroin without a licence or prescription are crimes in all states and territories of Australia. Penalties range from fines of $3000 and/or one year in prison for possession or fines up to $250,000 and up to 25 years imprisonment for commercial **drug trafficking**. Police in Victoria are assessing a cautionary scheme, whereby those caught for the first time using heroin are formally cautioned and then referred to a drug treatment centre.

Heavier penalties

Anti-drug laws in most countries carry more severe penalties for trafficking than for possession of drugs for personal use. In Britain, for example, the maximum sentence for possession of heroin is seven years' imprisonment, along with a fine. Trafficking convictions – including producing or smuggling, supply or intent to supply – can lead to a sentence of life imprisonment.

Police and government authorities agree that a large portion of crime, especially robbery, is drug-related. In 1994, Tony Blair – who was then Leader of the Opposition in Britain – estimated that drug abuse was behind £2 billion of the £4 billion of all property crime committed each year in England and Wales. Other authorities have argued with the way that he reached these figures, but the fact remains that heroin has much wider criminal effects than just possession and supply.

A UK police team smashes open the door of a suspected heroin dealer.

The Misuse of Drugs Act

As the old saying goes, ignorance is no defence in a court of law. In the case of heroin and most controlled drugs, the law in question is the Misuse of Drugs Act 1971, which divides drugs into three classes and gives guidelines for penalties. Class A drugs, which include cocaine, crack, heroin and LSD, are considered most serious and the penalty for supply can be life imprisonment.

Life with heroin

A person who has become **dependent** on heroin gradually comes to think of only two things – how to get hold of the drug and how best to get the heroin into the bloodstream fast. The fastest way – and one that 'loses' none of the heroin in the process – is by **injecting** it. In the distorted world of the dependent user, this experience is often compared to a life and death experience. As the drug is pumped in, the person sinks into a sense of **oblivion** that seems to be almost like dying. Then, when the drug takes effect, the user feels a sense of joyful relief that they are alive again.

Pitfalls

Injecting, of course, introduces a number of serious risks for the heroin user. The most dangerous come from using shared needles, which can lead to contracting **hepatitis** or the **HIV** virus. Hitting an artery – rather than a vein – is another, and people can lose a limb as a result. Those who inject want the drug to go through a vein into the heart, so that it mixes with the bloodstream.

If it goes into an artery, which carries oxygen-rich blood to limbs and other parts of the body, it robs cells at these 'destinations' of the oxygen they need to survive. Other problems are linked to mixing heroin and other drugs, such as alcohol. Such combinations can produce vomiting and suffocation if they lead to unconsciousness.

Dozens of disgarded needles paint a dismal picture of the life of a regular heroin user.

The repeated use of any drug leads to a strain on the liver, and since women's livers are smaller than men's they have more severe side-effects. Heroin also stops ovulation and many users go months without a period. If a heroin user does become pregnant, she often gives birth to baby who is underweight. There is also a higher risk that the baby will die within a week of birth. In addition, some babies born to heroin-dependent mothers show some signs of **withdrawal**.

Life with heroin

Lost Nirvana

Sometimes, the 'rich and famous' are drawn to heroin – despite knowing the risks. Kurt Cobain, lead singer of the grunge band Nirvana, is just such a person. Cobain was born near Seattle in 1967. His childhood was unhappy and was made worse when his parents divorced when he was nine. Cobain later used soft drugs to cope with his depression. Things seemed to improve in the late 1980s when he set up Nirvana. At first Cobain was able to project his **insecurities** and tension through songs like 'Smells like Teen Spirit'. The depression, however, resurfaced and Cobain looked for stability. He married fellow singer Courtney Love, but her influence was – if anything – even more unsettling. The couple drifted in and out of heavy heroin use, risking having their daughter taken into care. Cobain tried to stop his increasing use of heroin, but it felt like the only source of comfort in an increasingly difficult life. Things came to a head around 5 April 1994, when Cobain went into his garage, took a great deal of heroin and then killed himself with a shotgun blast.

An ex-user's story

Adam began dealing in cannabis when he was still at school. He viewed the experience as a big adventure, and enjoyed travelling to North Africa to get more supplies to import to Britain. The money he made enabled him to try other drugs, including LSD, cocaine and heroin. Most of his friends believed that he was only a casual user of these drugs, but behind the scenes Adam had become **dependent** on heroin.

Gradually he realized that the heroin habit was taking hold of him and although he wanted to quit, he felt he couldn't. It was only when he took a large amount of cocaine to overcome a heavy dose of heroin that he changed his mind. The combination of the drugs caused him to pass out and he didn't wake up for a full day. He acknowledged then that the heroin use was causing him to risk his life for no real purpose. He adds, 'When things like that started happening, I knew I had to do something.' In Adam's case that action was to enrol in the Narcotics Anonymous programme to deal with his dependence. He was able to overcome his dependence and is now the father of three children.

Treatment and counselling

There is no denying that it is difficult for an **addicted** heroin user to stop taking the drug. The process of **withdrawal** involves up to a week of physical discomfort. The flu-like symptoms are caused by the body coming to terms with the physical lack of heroin, and help to reverse most of the aspects of physical **dependence**. Some users are able to go through this period on their own, driven by the need to be 'clean'. Others need the support of friends, family or trained counsellors to help them. They probably also need to be removed from surroundings that involves heroin use.

Uplifting pursuits such as yoga and meditation are helpful in allowing a former heroin user to feel in control of their body.

Calling on others

Heroin users can turn to support groups, whether they need to overcome their lingering psychological dependence – after going through physical withdrawal – or to get support in actually coming off the drug. Although there is no easy solution to dependence, many groups base their treatment on the strategies used for people with alcohol dependency. Organizations such as Narcotics Anonymous call for **abstinence** as a first step. This is backed up with meetings with other dependent users, which builds up to a network of mutual help.

Another type of treatment, which is more common in the United States, is aimed at people who are still using heroin. It tries to find a way of replacing the heroin with methadone, another **opiate**, and lowering the doses in stages.

Methadone treatment has a number of advantages. First, by offering a source of drugs, it reduces crime. Second, it can be taken orally, so that it carries no risk of infection with **HIV** or **hepatitis**. Although some heroin users might find themselves using methadone for years, they argue that the drug is their only hope of ridding themselves of dependence.

The Swiss strategy

In 1994, the Swiss government began a two-pronged programme of dealing with heroin use. First, it aimed to reduce the risk of **overdose** and other health risks associated with **injecting**. Then it tried to tackle the problem of drug-related crime. The government actually imported 200 kilograms of heroin, which was then distributed, under strict supervision, to 1146 Swiss **addicts**. There was a small charge for each dose, but the heroin was free for those who could not afford it.

After three years the programme was declared a success by the World Health Organization. The levels of AIDS, hepatitis and other blood disorders had dropped sharply, and the number of drug-related deaths was cut by half. Two-thirds of the addicts had been involved in crime at the start – that figure dropped to just three per cent.

Treatment and counselling

The Bristol approach

The Bristol Drugs Project (BDP) is a community-based drugs charity in the British port of Bristol, where there has been serious concern about drugs such as heroin. It addresses the issue of drug abuse on a number of levels, starting with information and advice and continuing through coming off drugs and re-entering society. It is a **confidential** first point of contact for drug users or their families, providing information and advice about treatment. Special services single out young people, with both home visits and support at the local youth court. The SCORE scheme is a structured group programme for those who are battling with **dependency**. Some of these users are referred to a special drug service for **detoxification** and to find housing.

For those who have made the break from dependency, the BDP provides a follow-up support group called the Relapse Avoidance Programme, to help people stay off drugs. This programme ties in with a range of local links to provide ex-users with opportunities in education and employment.

Many clinics that provide methadone for registered addicts insist it is consumed on the premises.

Methadone misgivings

Although methadone can be effective in heroin treatment, it can generate problems of its own. It is even more **addictive** than heroin, produces longer **withdrawal** symptoms and leads to more deaths from **overdose** – nineteen times more, according to one study. In addition, the 'high' is considered boring, and some users top up the methadone with other drugs.

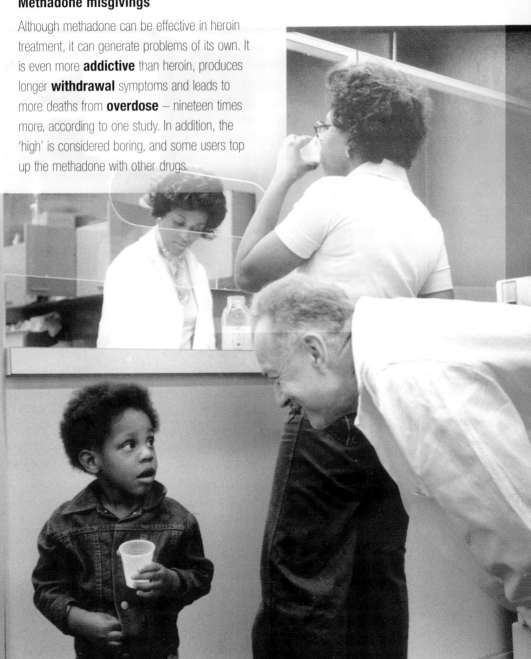

People to talk to

Over the years the world has learnt more about heroin, and how it affects people. Some of this information, such as that given in this book, puts heroin in its proper position as a drug that removes people from the 'real world' and can easily lead to a spiral of crime, ill health and even death.

Unfortunately, some of the information – such as the fact that you do not necessarily get hooked immediately the first time you take heroin – can get distorted as it is passed on by word of mouth. Young people may hear of people who can 'handle' heroin, even if this group is a small minority. They might even be dared to try the drug on this basis. This type of **peer pressure** is not helpful, but it is a strong and persuasive force.

Other voices

There are people who can put things in a different **perspective**, either by giving first-hand accounts of their own drug experiences or by outlining the clear dangers of heroin abuse. Parents and older family members are usually the best people to turn to first. If you feel uncomfortable talking about drugs with your parents and teachers, there are many alternative ways of getting information about heroin and other drugs.

The UK, like most countries, has a wide range of telephone contacts – many of them free of charge and most of them anonymous – where young people can find out more about heroin. Many of the organizations listed in the Information and advice section (pages 52–53) are specialist phone lines. They provide such a **confidential** telephone service, or they can suggest local agencies throughout the UK. Others are geared specifically to queries coming from younger people. Whether you approach one of these organizations, or a family member, a youth leader or teacher, the important thing is to be able to talk – and listen – freely about your drug concerns.

Telephone helpline volunteers are able to provide confidential advice to people with heroin problems.

Information and advice

We are well-served by organizations providing advice, counselling and other information relating to drug use. All of the contacts listed on these pages are helpful springboards for obtaining such advice or for providing confidential information telephone or by post.

Drug awareness contacts

ADFAM NATIONAL
Tel: 020 7928 8900
This is a national (UK) hotline for the friends and families of drug users. It provides confidential support and information to anyone who is worried about someone close to them who is using drugs.

British Association for Counselling (BAC), 1 Regent Place, Rugby CV21 2PJ, www.bac.co.uk
The BAC has an extensive directory of counselling services relating to drugs and other issues throughout the UK. Enquiries are by post only. Enclose an SAE for a list of counsellors in your area.

ISDD (Institute for the Study of Drug Dependence), Waterbridge House, 32–36 Loman Street, London SE1 0EE Tel: 020 7928 1211, www.isdd.co.uk
The ISDD has the largest drugs reference library in Europe and provides leaflets and other publications. SCODA (Standing Committee On Drug Abuse) is located at the same address (tel: 0207 928 9500) and is one of the best UK contacts for information on drugs.

Narcotics Anonymous, UK Service Office, PO Box 198J, London N19 3LS Tel: 020 7498 9904, www.ukna.org
Narcotics Anonymous (NA) is a network of self-help groups tackling the problem of drug dependence on the same lines as those of Alcoholics Anonymous.

National Drugs Helpline Tel: 0800 776600
The Helpline provides a free telephone contact for all aspects of drug use and has a database covering all of the British Isles for further information about specific drugs or regional information.

Release, Tel: 020 7603 8654 www.release.org.uk
Release operates a 24-hour helpline which provides advice on drug use and legal issues surrounding the subject.

Youth Access, 1A Taylors Yard, 67 Alderbrook Road, London SW12 8AD Tel: 020 8772 9900
Youth Access is an organization which refers young people to their local counselling service. It has a database of approximately 350 such services throughout the UK.

Contacts in the United States

Child Welfare League of America, 440 First Street NW, Washington, DC 20001, Tel: 202/638-2952 www.cwla.org
The Child Welfare League of America, based in Washington, provides useful contacts across the country in most topics relating to young people's problems, many of them related to drug involvement.

DARE America, PO Box 775, Dumfries, VA 22026, Tel: 703/860-3273
www.dare-america.com
Drug Abuse Resistance and Education (DARE) America is a national organization that links law-enforcement and educational resources to provide up-to-date and comprehensive information about all aspects of drug use.

Youth Power, 300 Lakeside Drive, Oakland, CA 94612, Tel: 510/451-6666, ext. 24
Youth Power is a nationwide organization involved in widening awareness of drug-related problems. It sponsors clubs and local affiliates across the country in an effort to help young people make their own sensible choices about drugs, and to work against the negative effects of peer pressure.

Contacts in Australia

ADCA, PO Box 269, Woden, ACT 2606
www.adca.org.au
The Alcohol and other Drug Council of Australia (ADCA), based in the Capital Territory, gives an overview of drug awareness organizations in Australia. Most of their work is carried out over the Internet but the postal address provides a useful link for those who are not 'on-line'.

Australian Drug Foundation, 409 King Street, West Melbourne, VIC 3003, Tel: 03 9278 8100
www.adf.org.au
The Australian Drug Foundation (ADF) has a wide range of information on all aspects of drugs, their effects and the legal position in Australia. It also provides handy links to state- and local-based drug organizations.

Centre for Education and Information on Drugs and Alcohol, Private Mail Bag 6 Rozelle, NSW 2039, Tel: 02 9818 0401
www.ceida.net.au
The Centre for Education and Information on Drugs and Alcohol is the ideal contact for information on drug programmes throughout Australia. It also has one of the most extensive libraries on drug-related subjects in the world.

Further reading

Buzzed, by Cynthia Kuhn, Scott Swartzwelder and Wilkie Wilson; New York and London: W.W. Norton and Company, 1998

Drugs, by Anita Naik, part of Wise Guides Series; London: Hodder Children's Books, 1997

Drugs and the Party Line, by Kevin Williamson; London: Rebel Inc., 1997

Drugs: The Facts, HEA leaflet; London: Health Education Authority, 1997 Drugs Wise, by Melanie McFadyean; Cambridge: Icon books, 1997

Street Drugs, by Andrew Tyler; London: Coronet, 3rd edition, 1995

Taking Drugs Seriously, A Parent's Guide to Young People's Drug Use, by Julian Cohen and James Kay; London: Thorsons, 1997

The Score: Facts about Drugs, HEA leaflet; London: Health Authority, 1998

Index

Titles in the *Need to Know* series include:

Hardback   0 431 09779 8

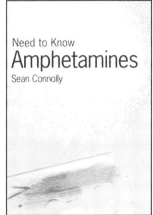

Hardback   0 431 09777 1

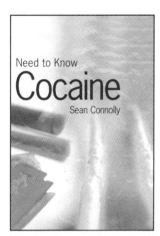

Hardback   0 431 09775 5

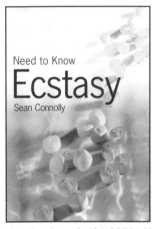

Hardback   0 431 09781 X

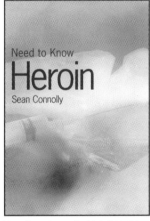

Hardback   0 431 09774 7

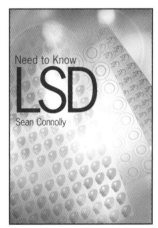

Hardback   0 431 09776 3

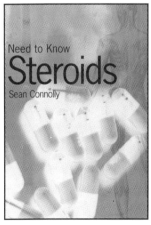

Hardback   0 431 09782 8

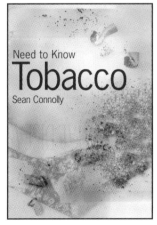

Hardback   0 431 09780 1

Find out about the other titles in this series on our website www.heinemann.co.uk/library